D0787473

PRINTMAKING SKILLS LAB

SARAH HODGSON

CRABTREE
PUBLISHING COMPANY
WWW.CRABTREEBOOKS.COM

ART SKILLS LAB

Author
Sarah Hodgson

Editors
Marcia Abramson, Reagan Miller

Photo research
Melissa McClellan

Cover/Interior Design
T.J. Choleva

Project Designer
Sarah Hodgson

Proofreader
Kathy Middleton

**Production coordinator
and Prepress technician**
Tammy McGarr

Print coordinator
Katherine Berti

Developed and produced for
Crabtree Publishing by
BlueApple*Works* Inc.

Consultant
Trevor Hodgson
Fine artist and former director of The Dundas Valley School of Art

Art & Photographs
Shutterstock.com: © Komsan Loonprom (cover middle right); © Excellent backgrounds (background); © Dmytro Vietrov (p. 4 left); FrameAngel (p. 5 right middle); © KOKTARO (p. 5 bottom left); © ETIENjones (p. 6 top left); © IPOP (p. 6 top middle); © Piyato (p. 6 middle left); © Be Good (p. 6 middle, middle); © ajt (p. 6 middle right); © chrisatpps (p. 6 bottom left); © Tabuda Y (p. 7 middle left);

© Austen Photography/Sarah Hodgson (cover, title page, TOC, p. 5, 7– 29)

Instructive paintings © Sarah Hodgson cover, p. 7– 29 excluding bios
p. 5 top Margret Hofheinz-Döring/Galerie Brigitte Mauch Göppingen/Creative Commons
p. 5 top left Charles Marion Russell/Library of Congress/Public Domain
p. 5 bottom right Albrecht Dürer/Metropolitan Museum of Art/Public Domain
p. 13 Paul Klee/Public Domain/The Museum of Modem Art
Digital Image © The Museum of Modem Art/Licensed by SCALA / Art Resource, NY
p. 15 Paul Gauguin/Public Domain
p. 17 © Sybil Andrews Estate/The Museum of Modem Art
Digital Image © The Museum of Modem Art/Licensed by SCALA / Art Resource, NY
p. 23 © Succession H. Matisse / SOCAN (2018)
Photo CJ'edit : Erich Lessing / Art Resource, NY
p. 27 Edgar Degas/Purchase, Mr. and Mrs. Richard J. Bernhard Gift, 1972
Metropolitan Museum of Art/Public Domain

Library and Archives Canada Cataloguing in Publication

Hodgson, Sarah, 1962-, author
        Printmaking skills lab / Sarah Hodgson.

(Art skills lab)
Includes index.
Issued in print and electronic formats.
ISBN 978-0-7787-5224-0 (hardcover).--
ISBN 978-0-7787-5237-0 (softcover).--
ISBN 978-1-4271-2181-3 (HTML)

        1. Prints--Technique--Juvenile literature. 2. Prints--Juvenile
literature. I. Title.

NE860.H62 2018   j760.28   C2018-905554-5
                                                        C2018-905555-3

Library of Congress Cataloging-in-Publication Data

Names: Hodgson, Sarah, 1962- author.
Title: Printmaking skills lab / Sarah Hodgson.
Description: New York, New York : Crabtree Publishing, [2019] |
    Series: Art skills lab | Includes index.
Identifiers: LCCN 2018050542 (print) | LCCN 2018056562 (ebook) |
    ISBN 9781427121813 (Electronic) |
    ISBN 9780778752240 (hardcover : alk. paper) |
    ISBN 9780778752370 (pbk. : alk. paper)
Subjects: LCSH: Prints--Technique--Juvenile literature. |
    Artists--Biography--Juvenile literature.
Classification: LCC NE860 (ebook) | LCC NE860 .H59 2019 (print) |
    DDC 769--dc23
LC record available at https://lccn.loc.gov/2018050542

Crabtree Publishing Company

www.crabtreebooks.com   1-800-387-7650

Printed in the U.S.A./012019/CG20181123

**Published in Canada
Crabtree Publishing**
616 Welland Ave.
St. Catharines, Ontario
L2M 5V6

**Published in the United States
Crabtree Publishing**
PMB 59051
350 Fifth Avenue, 59th Floor
New York, New York 10118

**Published in the United Kingdom
Crabtree Publishing**
Maritime House
Basin Road North, Hove
BN41 1WR

**Published in Australia
Crabtree Publishing**
Unit 3 – 5 Currumbin Court
Capalaba
QLD 4157

CONTENTS

GET INTO PRINTMAKING

Read this book with a sense of adventure! It is designed to unleash the creativity that exists within you! The projects in this book will help you express your feelings, your thoughts, and your ideas through your art. When learning to make prints, enjoy the process and don't worry too much about the finished product. To make it easier, all the projects in this book can be done by hand-pressing. Find your own individual style and run with it!

MINI-BIOGRAPHIES

Throughout the book you will find mini-biographies highlighting the work of well-known artists. You can learn a lot about printing **techniques** by looking at great works of art. Experiment with the techniques the artists used. Examine each artwork to see how its parts were put together, and how **symmetry**, types of lines, and color were used.

WHAT IS PRINTMAKING? ···○

Printmaking is the art of creating an image on one material and transferring it to another. The artist carves the image into the first material, which is called the **printing plate**. A plate can be made from wood, linoleum, cardboard, foam, or many other materials, including vegetables!

Next, the artist applies paint or ink to the plate. Paper or fabric is pressed against the plate so that the image is reproduced. Prints can be made by hand-pressing, as you will be doing, or by using a hand-powered printing press. Finally, the plate and the paper or fabric are separated.

Printing plates can be used over and over again. When professional artists make a batch, or series, of prints from one plate, they write the number of each one in pencil at the bottom of the print on the left. For example, print 2/15 means it is the second in a batch of 15 prints. The artist's name goes at the bottom on the right. The print title and date may be added as well.

MAIN TYPES OF PRINTMAKING

Prints can fall into one of several categories:

RELIEF PRINTING

A relief print is a raised image created on a flat surface. This is usually done by cutting away areas that are not part of the design. The raised areas, or ridges, are covered with ink or paint, but not the grooves. When it is printed, it is a mirror image of the design. The relief printing technique is similar to using a rubber stamp. The most popular examples of this style of printmaking are **woodcut** and **linocut**.

Bridge, linocut, 1960, by Margret Hofheinz-Döring

INTAGLIO

Intaglio means "**engraved** work" in Italian. The technique is the opposite of a relief print. A design is cut into the printing plate. Ink or paint is rubbed into the grooves, and the surface is wiped clean. Then a heavy press is used to transfer the image made by the inked grooves.

Today intaglio is used in printing currency, banknotes, and passports.

A 1903 lithograph by Charles Marion Russell shows *The Last Custer Fight in the American West*.

LITHOGRAPHY

In lithography, an image is created directly on a stone or metal printing plate using oily materials. The area around the design is treated with water-based materials. When ink or paint is applied, it sticks only to the design because oil and water do not mix. The plate is very durable and can make many prints. This technique, invented in 1796, is a popular form of printmaking today.

Screen printing does not require any type of press.

SERIGRAPHY (SCREEN PRINTING)

Serigraphy is a way to create an image by pressing ink through a fine screen which has some areas blocked off by a stencil. The stencil can be made from paper, fabric, plastic, or even leaves. This technique is also called **screen printing**.

ALBRECHT DÜRER

(1471 – 1528) Germany

Albrecht Dürer was a master of the woodcut, which is a type of relief printing. The first woodcuts were crude because it was difficult to carve hardwood. Dürer, however, was very skilled at painting and engraving. He used many different carving tools such as chisels, gouges, and knives to create fine lines and intricate details in his woodcuts. His work influenced many other artists.

Albrecht Dürer made woodcuts of coats of arms.

MATERIALS AND COLORS

All the projects in this book can be printed without a printing press. You will use your hands or a rolling pin to press and transfer the ink to the paper.

Applying ink or paint to a plate can be done with a brayer, which is a small rubber roller with a handle. If you don't have a brayer you can use a brush or sponge. It will be harder to get the ink perfectly smooth on the surface of the plate, but it can create interesting effects.

Brayer for applying ink

Printing ink can come in small tubes or large jars.

You can use soft rubber-like materials as printing surfaces that are easier and safer to cut than **linoleum**.

Acrylic paint comes in tubes or jars.

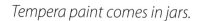

Tempera paint comes in jars.

Rolling pin

WHAT SURFACE TO PRINT ON?
You can use a variety of different materials for the background of your printmaking. The paper must be strong so it doesn't rip while printing. It should be absorbent so that the ink or paint can be transferred to the paper. It should be a heavyweight paper so it doesn't curl up and warp once the ink is applied. You can find printmaking paper in large sheets at art supply stores. You can also use watercolor paper.

Lino cutters come with a handle and a set of blades for making different size lines.

Caution
Use these tools with adult supervision and with great care.

6

USING COLOR IN PRINTMAKING

Artists use the color wheel as a tool to help them mix colors. A color wheel is a diagram that shows how colors are related. A simple color wheel is divided into two types of colors: primary and secondary. The **primary colors** are red, blue, and yellow. They are called primary because they are the only three colors that can't be made from combining other colors. **Secondary colors** are made by mixing two primary colors together.

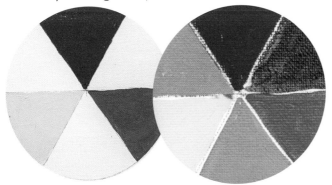

Draw your own color wheel to practice mixing colors. Mix red and yellow to create orange. Mix red and blue to create violet. Mix yellow and blue to create green.

COMPLEMENTARY COLORS

When choosing colors for a drawing, remember that colors from opposite sides of the wheel **complement**, or balance, each other. For example, red and green, yellow and violet, and blue and orange are complementary color pairs.

TINTS AND SHADES

Tints and shades are variations of a color. Using different tints and shades in printmaking creates visual interest. A color tint is created by mixing white ink with a color. A color shade is created by adding black ink to a color. If you add both black and white ink to a color, you will create a **neutral color.**

Tint *Color + white*   Shade *Color + black*

DESIGN ELEMENTS IN PRINTMAKING

What makes a print interesting? It will depend on the creative use of the elements of design: line, shape, pattern, texture, and composition.

Line is the edge between two colors or shapes. It does not have to be straight! Lines can go in any direction and be any shape, length, or thickness. Artists use lines to draw the viewer's eye in the direction they want it to go.

Shape is any enclosed space in a print. A shape's edges may be created by lines, textures, or colors.

Pattern is the way colors or shapes are combined and repeated to create a special effect.

Texture is how the surface of the artwork feels or looks.

Composition is the arrangement of all the shapes, lines, colors, spaces, and textures in an image. Artists carefully place these elements so that the viewers' eyes will follow a path leading to the key element or message of the work.

STAMPING

Stamping is a form of relief printmaking. To make a stamp, first draw your image on solid material such as wood, rubber block, linoleum, or foam. Then start carving or cutting away the areas that you don't want to show. By adding ink or paint to the block's raised surface or ridges, you can transfer your art to another surface. The carved-out areas, or the grooves, will not print. There are many ways to create stamps. In this exercise, you will create your own stamps with craft foam. Simple shapes work best with a solid block of color. Foam stamps are a great way to make a number of prints at the same size and shape.

You Will Need:
- Foam sheets
- Scissors
- Pencil
- Glue gun or white glue
- Paint brush or roller
- Palette or scrap paper
- Acrylic paints or block printing inks
- Large paper

PROJECT GUIDES

1   Draw the shapes for your print onto the foam. Use scissors to carefully cut them out.

2   Cut out squares of foam that are bigger than the shapes. Glue the shapes to the squares. If you use white glue instead of a glue gun, you must wait longer for the glue to dry.

3   Add a small blob of paint to a scrap paper or a palette, which is a surface to mix paints on. Dip your roller or brush in the paint. Apply paint to the shape making sure it is fully covered. Try not to get paint on the square backing of your stamp.

4   Place your foam shape onto the paper and press firmly with the palm of your hand. Carefully lift the stamp straight up to avoid getting extra paint on the paper.

5   Continue to print all the shapes you have made. You can create a pattern by alternating stamps.

GEOMETRIC ART

Toothpicks are a great tool for making **geometric shapes**. Create toothpick printing stamps and try experimenting with lines and angles.

You Will Need:

- Foam sheets
- Scissors
- Toothpicks
- Glue gun
- Paintbrush
- Acrylic paints
- Large piece of paper

1 Cut several square pieces of foam. On each square, arrange toothpicks in geometric shapes, such as squares, triangles, and other polygons. Glue the toothpicks to the foam with a glue gun. To create shapes with thicker lines, glue two toothpicks side by side.

2 Use a paintbrush to cover the toothpicks with paint. Be careful not to get too much paint on the foam.

3 Place your toothpick block on the paper and apply a bit of pressure using the palm of your hand. Lift off the block carefully and continue to print more of the same geometric shape.

4 Print a variety of different shapes. You can overlap some of the shapes. This will highlight the elements of space and line in your print.

Try This!

Foam stamps are a great way to create your own wrapping paper! Try stamping on brown or colored paper.

9

PRINT YOUR FRUITS AND VEGGIES

Vegetables and fruits can make great stamps for printing. Some fruits and vegetables make unusual shapes, such as star fruit or a leafy vegetable called radicchio. You can make large pieces of art using bright colors with fruit and veggie stamps.

You Will Need:
- Variety of fruits and vegetables
- Kitchen knife
- Acrylic paints or block printing inks
- Palette or scrap paper
- Paintbrush or roller
- Large paper

PROJECT GUIDES

1 Choose several fruits and vegetables to use for printing. Fruits and vegetables that are firm make the best stamps.

2 Cut the fruits and vegetables in half so that they have a flat surface.

3 Add a small blob of acrylic paint or block printing ink to your palette or a scrap paper. Dip your roller or brush in the paint. Paint or roll the flat surface of your fruit or vegetable stamp.

4 Press your fruit or vegetable stamp onto a clean sheet of paper. A repeated pattern can be created by alternating stamps on the paper.

5 Experiment with colors and their relationships according to the color wheel on page 7. For example, choose colors that are complementary, such as blue and orange. The examples shown here include orange, blue, black, red, and green and stamps made from apples, oranges, radicchio, and carrots.

6 Try overlapping stamps to create layers.

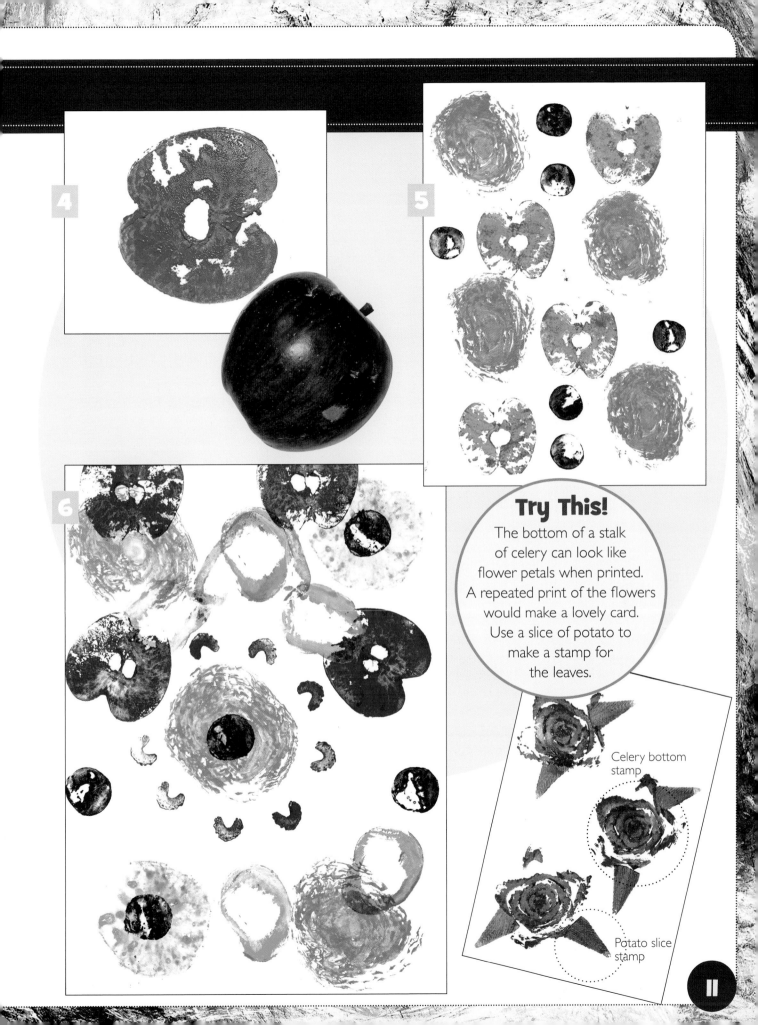

4

5

6

Try This!

The bottom of a stalk of celery can look like flower petals when printed. A repeated print of the flowers would make a lovely card. Use a slice of potato to make a stamp for the leaves.

Celery bottom stamp

Potato slice stamp

TEXTURED STAMPING

Stamps made from materials found around your house can add great texture to your prints. Ideal items have patterns and can feel smooth, rough, soft, or hard. Try overlapping shapes, textures, and colors to create a design.

You Will Need:

- Variety of textures
- Wooden blocks for solid shapes
- Cardboard scraps
- Wood scraps
- Old thread spools
- Glue gun
- Paintbrush or roller
- Acrylic paints
- Large paper

PROJECT GUIDES

1 Collect a variety of items with interesting textures. You can use string, rubber bands, buttons, bubble wrap, wooden blocks, and any other interesting items you find.

2 Create printing blocks by gluing each of your textured items to a wooden block. You can also create a texture block by gluing a button to an empty spool of thread. Children's blocks may be used as well. The edge of a piece of cardboard can be used to make straight lines on your print.

3 Using a paintbrush or roller, apply acrylic paint to the item on your texture block.

4 Press the block onto your paper. Put some light pressure on the block using the palm of your hand. Start at the bottom of your paper and work your way up, alternating your blocks.

5 Changing a block's position and direction can create interesting prints. Try overlapping your blocks and adding lines using cardboard edges.

1
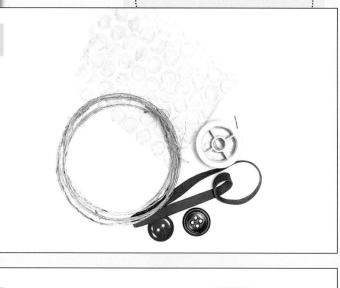

2
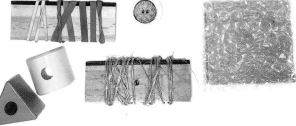

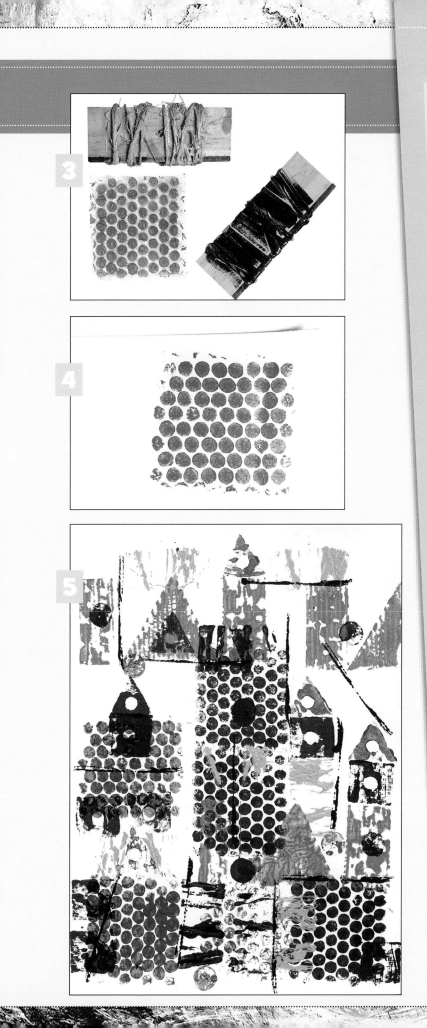

3

4

5

(1879 – 1940) Switzerland

Artist Paul Klee used geometric shapes and bold colors to represent emotions and ideas. Colored rectangles or squares, sometimes overlapping, are the building blocks for many of his famous works. His paintings, prints, and **etchings** often have a dreamlike or childlike quality. Klee was also a musician. Some of his works include symbols that look like musical notes.

Created in 1923, Klee's *Sublime Side* lithograph was used as a postcard for an art show.

IMPRESSIVE FOAM

A drawing has two kinds of space. **Positive space** is the area that contains the subject or subjects of the drawing. **Negative space** is the rest of the area around or between subjects, or between a subject and the edge of the page. Positive and negative space are shapes that interact with each other. In this exercise, you will carve your subject into a foam plate and paint the negative space around it with a color. When you press the plate onto the page, the negative space of your drawing on the plate will become the positive space of the print.

You Will Need:

- Styrofoam plate or container
- Pencil
- Paintbrush or roller
- Acrylic paints or block printing inks
- Large paper

PROJECT GUIDES

1 Cut out a flat rectangle from a Styrofoam plate or container.

2 Use a sharp pencil to draw or write a word that you wish to print. Make sure the lines you draw are pressed deep into the foam for best results. You could write a word that has meaning to you or use your name. If you use a word, it must be written as a **mirror image** of the word in order to be the right way around when you print it.

3 Roll or paint the acrylic or block printing ink onto your rectangle.

4 Use a clean sheet of paper to print on. Place the painted rectangle onto the paper and press firmly but not hard enough to break the Styrofoam. To make sure the plate is not upside down, mark the top and bottom of the rectangle on the back.

5 If you want, you can repeat the image all over your paper. You can do one color, or wash your plate and do several colors.

3

4

5

(1848–1903) France

Paul Gauguin liked to shake up his life and his art. He traveled as far as Tahiti in search of a simple life and harmony with nature. These were themes he used in his art. Gauguin tried many types of art, including painting, printmaking, and ceramics. For his woodcuts, he used a needle, a small engraving tool, and a pocket knife to make different types of lines. He also sanded the wood to get unusual effects, textures, colors, and accidental markings. It gave a mysterious, dreamlike quality to his images.

This 1899 woodcut was hand-printed for a magazine cover.

Try This!

Try experimenting with different tools to make indentations in foam. A plastic knife could be used to make wider lines. A toothpick could be used to make small lines. Try filling in large areas with lines, like Paul Gauguin did in the woodcut pictured above.

CARVING LINO

A linocut, like a woodcut, is a type of relief printing. Instead of using a block of wood, the artist makes the printing plate from a piece of flooring called linoleum. It is a softer material than wood and used to be used as kitchen flooring. It can be carved easily with a sharp knife, a V-shaped chisel, or a **gouge**. Because it is easy to work with, linoleum is great for making both simple and detailed designs. Warning: This activity requires careful supervision by an adult.

You Will Need:
- Paper
- Pencil
- Soft linoleum block
- Linoleum carving tool and a variety of gouges
- Block printing inks
- Roller or paintbrush

PROJECT GUIDES

1. Draw your design on paper first. Put your linoleum block on the paper and use a pencil to trace around its edges. This will help you plan the size of your design.

2. Redraw your design on the piece of soft linoleum. To help you know where to carve, use a pencil to shade the areas that you plan to cut out.

3. The carving tool for linoleum has different size gouges. Use the appropriate gouge for the area you are carving out. Be careful—gouges are very sharp. It is always safer to cut away from your body. Take your time during this part of the activity. If you make a mistake, make it part of your design. Think about creating texture as you carve.

4. When you are finished, use a roller to roll your block printing ink onto the front of your soft linoleum block. The parts that you cut will have no ink in them. Only the uncut parts will have ink on them.

5. Prepare a clean sheet of paper to print your linoleum block on. Place your linoleum block onto the paper and press firmly. Sometimes it helps to rub the back of a spoon across the back of the linoleum.

6. You can make a single print or repeat it to make a pattern.

4

5

6

(1898–1992) Great Britain/Canada

Sybil Andrews built airplanes and ships as a welder during WWI and WWII. She was fascinated by the way things move. In her linocuts, she laid forms and figures over each other to show machines, people, or animals in motion. She also used simple shapes and flat, bold colors to achieve a modern look.

Racing was printed in 1934.

Try This!

Try creating a series of five prints from one linocut. Use a pencil to sign your name on the bottom right, and number the prints at the bottom left of the paper. Number like this: 1/5, 2/5, 3/4, 4/5, and 5/5. You can add a title in the middle. All the prints should look as alike as you can make them.

LEAF IT

Leaves and other objects found in nature can be used in printmaking, too. Rubbing is one of the oldest forms of printmaking. To make a rubbing, you put paper or cloth over an object that has raised parts, or ridges. To capture the image of the item underneath, rub a pencil or crayon over the paper or cloth.

You Will Need:

- Variety of leaves
- Piece of **plexiglass**
- Roller or paintbrush
- Ink or acrylic paints
- Cotton swab
- Sponge or spray bottle
- Drawing paper

PROJECT GUIDES

1. Collect a variety of leaves that are different in size and shape.

2. Place a blob of ink on a piece of plexiglass. Use a roller to roll out a rectangle in the paint. Leave a border where you can hold the plexiglass. Make the border thin.

3. Arrange a variety of leaves on top of the plexiglass to create an interesting design. Press down and smooth the leaves with your fingers. Be careful because they are delicate. Using a bit of ink or paint on the end of a cotton swab, rub a darker shade of the background color on top of the leaves.

4. Using either a sponge or a spray bottle, dampen a sheet of drawing paper with water. (This helps the ink transfer.) Place the paper on top of the plexiglass. Press down with your hands and rub the paper. You can also roll a rolling pin over the paper to increase the pressure.

5. Slowly pull the paper away from the plexiglass. Let it dry.

Try This!

Collect more leaves. Paint the leaves using acrylic paint and a brush. Prepare a clean sheet of paper to print on. Lay a leaf on the paper and gently press the back of the leaf with your fingers. Carefully remove the leaf. Next, add a new leaf in a different color. Layer the leaves to create new colors where they overlap. Add another leaf and a third color. Continue until you are happy with the design.

SHAPE COLLOGRAPHY

Collography is a form of printmaking that involves making a print of a **collage** made of textured materials. The plate and paper are pressed together in a printing press or by hand. The resulting print is called a collagraph. In this exercise, you will make a printing plate using cardboard glued on another piece of cardboard, and print your design on two different backgrounds.

You Will Need:
- Cardboard (3 pieces)
- Drawing paper
- Scissors
- Masking tape
- Ink or acrylic paint
- Roller
- Glue gun or glue
- Paintbrush

PROJECT GUIDES

1. Find two pieces of cardboard that are the same size. Cut two sheets of drawing paper the same size as the cardboard. In the example shown, a standard size of 8.5 × 11 inches (22 × 28 cm) has been used. Have a third piece of cardboard of any size ready for cutting out the shapes for your printing plate design.

2. Cover one of the two matching pieces of cardboard with masking tape. Wrap the ends over the back of the cardboard. Change directions with the tape to create an interesting textured pattern.

3. Place a few blobs of ink or paint on the taped board. Roll the paint around with a roller until the whole board is covered. Lay a damp piece of drawing paper on top of the board. Rub all over with your hands to press the paper to the board. Pull the paper from the board and let it dry. Apply more ink or paint to the cardboard and print another sheet.

4. Cut shapes out of the third piece of cardboard. Glue the shapes to the second piece of matching cardboard.

5. Use a paintbrush to cover the shapes with ink or paint.

6. Place your cardboard printing plate onto one of the background sheets and press down. Rub all over with your hands to press the plate to the background sheet. Turn it over and pull the sheet from the printing plate. Let it dry. Repeat with your other background sheet.

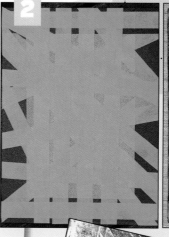

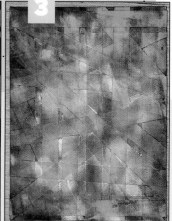

Background prints

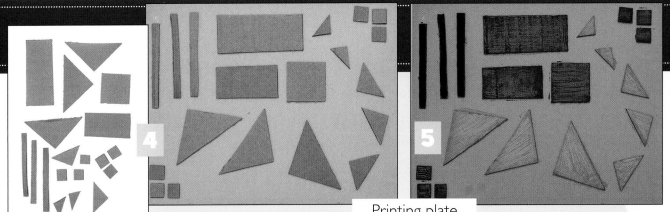

4

5

Printing plate

6

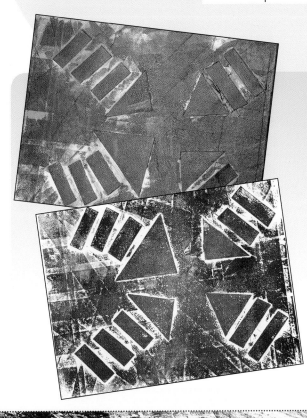

Final prints

Try This!

Instead of creating a collograph in two steps, try printing the background and image at the same time. The main difference is that you won't be able to make different colored backgrounds like you can with the two-step process.

For this method, you will need a thin cardboard like a cereal box. Cut the shapes and glue them to the taped cardboard as explained in Step 4. Ink or paint the entire board with a roller. Reverse the printing process. Put a damp paper on top of your printing plate, press hard, and **pull a print**. You can repeat the inking or painting to make another.

POCHOIR

People have been making art with stencils as far back as early humans, who traced their hands on cave walls. *Pochoir* is the French word for stencil. The technique was developed in France in the 1800s. It is a method of stenciling that produces images that look freshly printed and vibrant. Many artists use the pochoir technique to make prints for book illustrations.

You Will Need:

- Heavy white paper
- Pencil
- Scissors
- Sponge
- Acrylic paint

PROJECT GUIDES

1. Create three stencil shapes. Draw your shapes on a piece of heavy white paper.

2. Cut out each shape in a square.

3. Carefully cut the image out of each shape with scissors. Start inside the image so you don't cut into the negative space around the image.

4. Place your stencil on your paper. Using a sponge and acrylic paint, carefully dab the color inside your stencil. Hold the stencil in place while applying the paint.

5. Repeat your stencil print around your paper, creating a pattern to fill the space. Let the paint dry before moving on to the next stencil shape.

6. Once the paint is dry after using the first stencil, you can repeat steps 4 and 5 with the second stencil. You can overlap the shapes, making new colors where the shapes overlap. Let the paint dry.

7. Repeat steps 4 and 5 with your third stencil to add more prints.

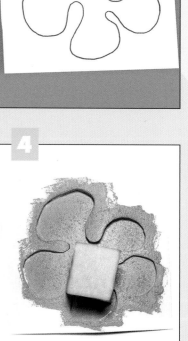

5

6

7

(1869–1954) France

Artist Henri Matisse used pochoir to create bold, colorful prints. In 1947, he published *Jazz*, a book of pochoir prints. Matisse appreciated the musical form of jazz for its creativity and imaginative, free-flowing form. He wanted his pochoir prints in the book to take on these same characteristics.

Icarus, from *Jazz*, 1947

Try This!

A famous quote of Henri Matisse was, "There are always flowers for those who want to see them." What do you think he meant by that? Create a stencil print to illustrate the quote.

23

SCREEN PRINTING

Silk screening or screen printing is often used in making posters or T-shirts. It is a great way to produce large numbers of identical prints on paper or fabric. Screen prints are made by forcing paint through a tightly stretched screen. The artist makes a drawing on the screen, then paints around it with a substance, such as glue. After it dries, the screen is used as a stencil. The first screens were made of silk giving the technique its name.

You Will Need:
- Paper and pencil
- Scissors
- Old nylons or pantyhose
- Embroidery hoop
- Permanent marker
- Mod Podge
- Painter's tape or masking tape
- Brushes
- Acrylic paint
- Old plastic gift card

PROJECT GUIDES

1. On paper, draw a design you would like for a silk-screen print. Keep the design simple with larger shapes and spaces between the shapes.

2. Cut one leg off a pair of pantyhose with scissors, then cut longways down the leg so it unfolds into one layer of nylon. Stretch the nylon in an embroidery hoop, and cut off the edges that hang out the sides.

3. Place your drawing under the hoop. Using a permanent marker, trace your drawing onto the nylon.

4. Now you need to block out the areas where you don't want any color to print. Turn the hoop fabric-side up. Use pieces of masking tape to cover the space around your design. Be sure to include the space between the design and the border.

5. Brush Mod Podge to the edge of the lines of your design. Let it dry. Look carefully for areas you missed and coat them with Mod Podge again if necessary.

6. Use one color of acrylic paint to create your design. An old plastic gift card works well to apply the paint evenly over your design. Turn the hoop fabric-side down so that it lays flat against the paper. Apply a line of paint at the top of the taped area and drag it across the nylon using the card. Repeat this dragging step two to three times, starting from the top of your design and pulling down.

7. Quickly lift the embroidery hoop off your paper. You can continue to repeat this design on more sheets of paper.

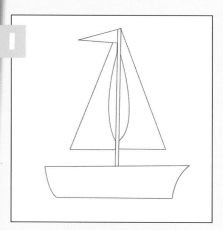

Pull nylon over first piece of hoop

Place second hoop on top

Cut away the nylon edges

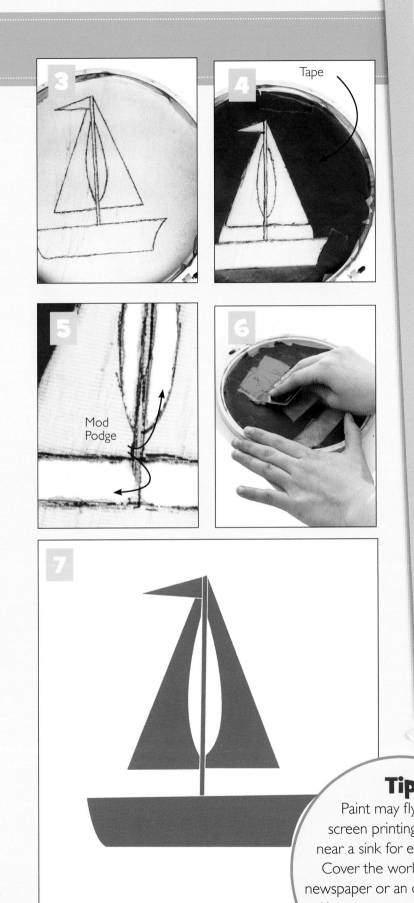

3

4

Tape

5

Mod Podge

6

7

Try This!

Silks screening is a fantastic way to create several T-shirts with the same design. Using acrylic paint will prevent your design from fading when you wash your T-shirts.

- Wash and dry your T-shirt in the laundry to prepare it for printing.

- Follow the instructions on page 24 to prepare your nylon silk screen.

- Cut a large piece of cardboard that fits inside the T-shirt. The cardboard will block any paint from reaching the back of your T-shirt.

- Place your design in the embroidery hoop so that it lays flat against the T-shirt.

- Apply a line of paint just above your design. Use your plastic gift card to drag the paint down over your design. Repeat this dragging step two to three times. Be sure to always start at the top and drag the paint down over the design.

- Quickly lift off the embroidery hoop and let your T-shirt dry. If you like, you can continue to make several T-shirts with the same design.

Tip

Paint may fly during screen printing, so work near a sink for easy cleanup. Cover the work area with newspaper or an old tablecloth. Keep paper towels or rags within reach. Wear old clothes!

25

ONE OF A KIND

Monotype printmaking is a technique that creates one-of-a-kind prints. Using ink or paint, the artist draws on a polished surface, such as glass, metal, or stone. When absorbent paper is pressed on top of the drawing, the design transfers in a mirror image. The paper picks up most of the paint or ink, so there is not enough for another print. As a result, the print is unique. If you do press another sheet of paper on the inked surface, you will get a faint image which is known as a ghost print.

You Will Need:

- Photo or drawing
- Paper
- Scissors
- Tape
- Ink or acrylic paint
- Roller or brush
- Piece of plexiglass
- Dull pencil

PROJECT GUIDES

1. Choose your subject. For this type of printmaking a simple subject with not too much detail will work best. Think of something that can be illustrated with an outline and a few defining marks such as an animal or flower. Find photos to trace.

2. You can either photocopy your photos or print copies of digital photos onto regular paper. Cut them out. Tape the photo onto a piece of drawing paper that is slightly larger than the photo.

3. Use a roller or a brush to spread a thin layer of ink or paint on the piece of plexiglas. Make sure your paint area is about the same size as your drawing paper. Let it dry for about 10 minutes.

4. Place your drawing paper on top of the ink on the plexiglass with the picture side facing up. Tape the paper to the glass. Use a dull pencil to trace around the subject in your photo. Do the outside outline first. Trace inside details next. Try not to rest your hand on the plexiglass while tracing. Trace around the outside of the photo to make a frame for the print. Slowly and carefully pull the paper away from the plexiglass. Let it dry.

5. To make another print, take your brush or roller and smooth over the image created in the ink. If the ink or paint is too dry add a couple of drops of water.

6. Make another print using the same photo or a different one. Even if you use the same photo, each print will be different.

1

2

3

Tip
While working you can carefully pull the photo up a little bit to make sure you are pressing hard enough with the pencil.

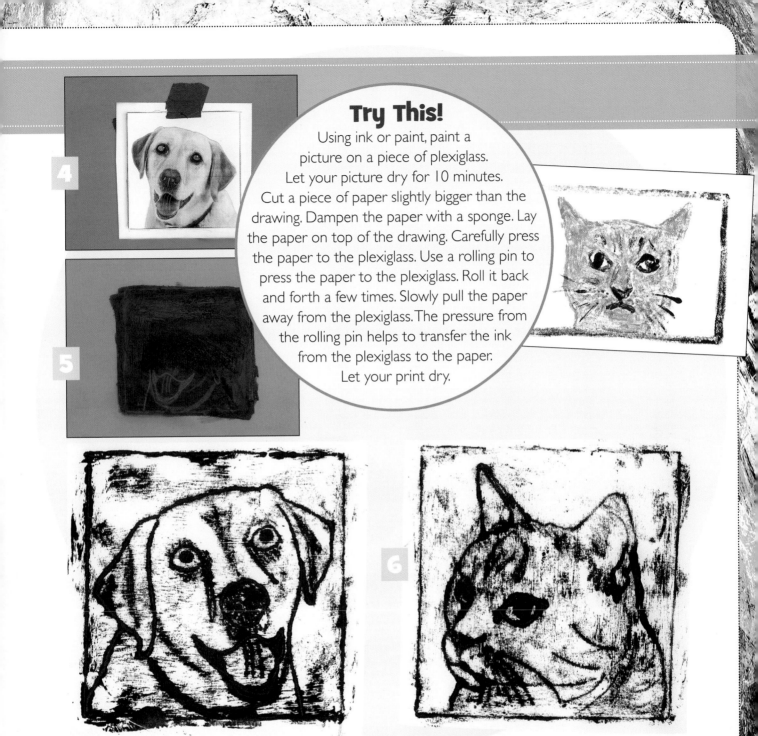

4

5

6

Try This!

Using ink or paint, paint a picture on a piece of plexiglass. Let your picture dry for 10 minutes. Cut a piece of paper slightly bigger than the drawing. Dampen the paper with a sponge. Lay the paper on top of the drawing. Carefully press the paper to the plexiglass. Use a rolling pin to press the paper to the plexiglass. Roll it back and forth a few times. Slowly pull the paper away from the plexiglass. The pressure from the rolling pin helps to transfer the ink from the plexiglass to the paper. Let your print dry.

EDGAR DEGAS

(1834–1917) France

Edgar Degas was a French Impressionist painter known primarily for paintings and drawings of dancers. Degas was inspired by a trip to Burgundy, France, to create a series of landscape monotypes in 1890. He wanted to capture the feeling of rolling through the misty countryside in a carriage. He called these works "imaginary landscapes." He used oil paints and oil pastels on a smooth surface to create his monotypes.

Landscape, 1892.

PUT IT ALL TOGETHER

Different types of printmaking can be used together to make a unique work of art. Using the techniques you have learned, you can create a print that demonstrates your understanding of printmaking. Choose from the following techniques: stamping, foam printing, linocut, rubbing, collography, stencil printing, screen printing, and monotype printmaking.

You Will Need:

● The materials will be different depending on the types of prints you will combine. Refer to the material list in the projects in this book.

PROJECT GUIDES

1 Choose three methods of printing that you have learned using the projects in this book. The example shown here uses stencil printing, rubbing, and foam stamping.

2 Gather your supplies. You can use stamps you have already made or make new ones.

3 Prepare your paper. If your images are different sizes, start with the largest first. Here, we did the stencil of the bird first using acrylic paint and a sponge.

4 Start to add your other designs to fill the space. The example shows leaf prints below the bird.

5 Finally the heart foam stamps are added above the bird. Remember to consider overlapping to add space and new colors to your design.

Try This!

This exercise combines three printing techniques. Try making a print using every technique in the book. Use silk screening as the first technique and then build upon it.

1

2

Books

Art Lab for Kids,
by Susan Schwake, Quarry Books, 2012.

Printmaking,
by Dana Meachen Rau, Cherry Lake
Publishing, 2015.

The Usborne Complete Book of Art Ideas,
by Fiona Watt, Usborne Publishing, 2011.

Maker Projects for Kids Who Love Printmaking,
by Joan Marie Galat, Crabtree Publishing
Company, 2017.

Websites

National Gallery of Art
https://www.nga.gov/education/kids.html
NGAkids Art Zone includes descriptions of interactive art-making tools that are free to download. You can also explore the collection of the National Gallery.

Painting for Kids
https://artfulparent.com/painting-activities-kids-60-ideas/
This site provides ideas for painting projects including painting large artworks and using unusual tools.

Kids View of Printmaking at The Tate
https://www.tate.org.uk/kids/explore/kids-view/meet-printmaker
This site provides a great introduction to printmaking as well as a wonderful collection of quizzes, art activities, and artist's biographies.

Toytheater
http://toytheater.com/doodle-pad/
Create digital art with a doodle pad. You can take a screenshot if you really like your creation.

GLOSSARY

collage A creative work made of various materials, such as paper, cloth, or wood, that are glued onto a surface

complement To complete or make better by providing something additional

engraved Something made by a printmaking technique that involves making cuts in a metal plate, which are filled with ink to create the image

etching A printmaking technique that uses chemicals to cut lines into a metal plate

geometric shapes Shapes made out of points and lines, such as triangles or squares

gouge A metal tool with a sharp, curved end

intaglio Any printmaking technique in which lines are cut into a printing plate

linocut A type of relief printing using a the printing plate carved from a piece of flooring material called linoleum

linoleum A type of flooring that is made from natural materials and comes in thin sheets; it is also used to make linocuts

mirror image An identical image, although reversed, such as a reflection in a mirror.

negative space The space around and between subjects in an artwork or photo

neutral color A color, such as gray, that is produced by mixing complementary colors; also called earth tones

plexiglass Transparent or see-through plastic often used in place of glass

positive space The area that contains the subject or subjects in an artwork or photo

primary colors Red, yellow, and blue, which are the colors from which any other color can be made

printing plate A piece of material that holds a design that will be reproduced

pull a print To make an image from a plate on paper or fabric

screen printing A printmaking technique that uses a stencil and a piece of tightly pulled fabric or mesh to reproduce an image

secondary colors Colors that result from mixing two primary colors

symmetry A state of balance among the elements of an artwork

techniques The ways in which things are done to accomplish a goal

woodcut A print made by using a block of wood as the printing plate

INDEX

ABOUT THE AUTHOR

Sarah Hodgson has a Fine Art degree and an Education degree. She began her teaching career at the Dundas Valley School of Art and has been teaching art, media arts, and animation in schools for more than twenty years. Her original art appears in many children's arts and crafts books.